MUSICIANS and THEIR INSPIRATIONS

HARRY STYLES and MICK JAGGER

Music and Style Icons

Tim Cooke

Lerner Publications ◆ Minneapolis

Lerner Publications Company
An imprint of Lerner Publishing Group, Inc.
241 First Avenue North
Minneapolis, MN 55401 USA

For reading levels and more information, look up this title at www.lernerbooks.com.

Main body text set in Eurostile LT Pro.
Typeface provided by Linotype.

Library of Congress Cataloging-in-Publication Data

Names: Cooke, Tim, 1961- author.
Title: Harry Styles and Mick Jagger : music and style icons / Tim Cooke.
Description: Minneapolis : Lerner Publications, 2024. | Series: Musicians and their inspirations | Includes bibliographical references and index. | Audience: Ages 8-12 | Audience: Grades 4-6 | Summary: "Harry Styles is a big fan of Mick Jagger. From music to fashion to breaking down social barriers, Styles takes inspiration from Jagger. Young readers learn more about their music and lives"— Provided by publisher.
Identifiers: LCCN 2023046261 (print) | LCCN 2023046262 (ebook) | ISBN 9798765626689 (library binding) | ISBN 9798765629093 (paperback) | ISBN 9798765635681 (epub)
Subjects: LCSH: Styles, Harry, 1994---Juvenile literature. | Jagger, Mick—Juvenile literature. | Singers—England—Biography—Juvenile literature. | Rock musicians—England—Biography—Juvenile literature. | LCGFT: Biographies.
Classification: LCC ML3930.S89 C66 2024 (print) | LCC ML3930.S89 (ebook) | DDC 782.42166092/2 [B]—dc23/eng/20231003

LC record available at https://lccn.loc.gov/2023046261
LC ebook record available at https://lccn.loc.gov/2023046262

Manufactured in the United States of America

1 - CG - 7/15/24

TABLE OF CONTENTS

Introduction

In April 2017, fans of Harry Styles and Mick Jagger got a big surprise. Styles had just split from his band One Direction. He was making his first solo appearance. He chose to appear on the popular late-night comedy show *Saturday Night Live*. Styles decided to dress as his idol, Mick Jagger. Jagger is the lead singer of the Rolling Stones. The band has been together for a long time.

Harry Styles has been a fan of Mick Jagger since the start of his musical career.

Mick Jagger is famous for the expressions he makes while he sings.

Styles dressed like Jagger did when he was younger. He leapt around the TV studio just like Jagger does on stage. He even copied Jagger's accent. It comes from southeast London, England. Jagger said he thought Styles's impression of him was funny. But Styles didn't get everything right. "I used to wear a lot more eye make-up than him," said Jagger.

CHAPTER 1

Starting Out

Jagger's and Styles's careers started in very different ways. Jagger started a band with a friend. Styles got placed in a band on a TV singing competition. But both had a love for music.

The Rolling Stones started with a chance meeting in 1962. Mick Jagger was waiting for a train near his home in Dartford, southeast London, England. He bumped into his childhood friend, Keith Richards. The two hadn't seen each other for a while. Jagger was holding some blues records he got from the United States. Richards wanted to know all about them. The two friends started to hang out together to listen to music.

Jagger has been friends with guitarist Keith Richards (left) for over sixty years. They enjoy the same kind of music.

Styles (right) joined One Direction in 2011 after appearing on a TV talent show.

Jagger and guitarist Ronnie Wood perform with the Rolling Stones in Milan, Italy.

Famous Band

Jagger and Richards started a band, the Rolling Stones. They played a kind of music that was unusual in Great Britain: the blues. By 1965, the five-member band had hit the big time. Only the Beatles were more famous than the Rolling Stones.

Jagger was the lead singer. He soon became known for his energetic dancing on stage. He had long hair and often wore makeup and tight clothes, which some people thought was shocking. Since their first hits, the Rolling Stones have sold more than 200 million records. They are still performing on stage.

TV Debut

Harry Styles first appeared on the British TV talent show *The X Factor*. He wasn't picked by the judges, but he did get a recall to the show. This time, he was part of a five-member group.

The group became One Direction. They finished third in the competition. Their first album was released in 2011. It made number one on the *Billboard* 200 chart. The band's next four albums were also successful. One Direction became one of the biggest boy bands in the world.

One Direction performs on The X Factor.

COOL CONNECTIONS

Styles and Jagger have both appeared in movies as actors. Jagger played the lead in a 1970 crime film. Styles has acted in movies such as *Dunkirk* and Marvel's *The Eternals*.

Styles (top left) prepares to film a scene in the 2017 movie Dunkirk.

In 2016, the boys of One Direction decided to take a break. Styles used the break to launch his solo career. In 2017, he released his debut single, "Sign of the Times." Since then, Styles has become one of the most successful solo singers in the world. His albums go straight to number one in the charts.

Harry Styles is known for his gender-fluid fashion choices.

INSPIRING THE INSPIRATION

LITTLE RICHARD

Rock and roll singer Little Richard inspired a teenage Mick Jagger with his energy. Jagger was such a big fan that he managed to get the Rolling Stones picked as the opening act for Little Richard when he toured England in October 1963. Little Richard remained a lifelong influence on Jagger.

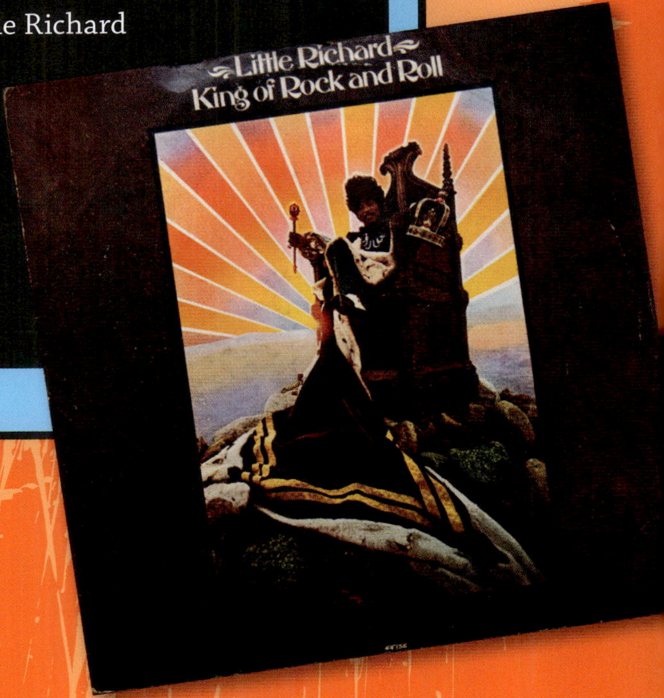

CHAPTER 2

Hit Writers

Both Jagger and Styles write their own songs. They're among the most successful songwriters of all time.

Mick Jagger and Keith Richards started writing together in 1965 for the Rolling Stones. Their first big hit was "(I Can't Get No) Satisfaction," which hit number one in July 1965. Since then, they have written dozens of hit songs.

Musical Process

Jagger often writes lyrics in a notebook. Then he tries out melodies on the guitar or the piano. He likes to work with a drummer to help him find a beat.

Jagger can also use a computer to give him the drumbeat. He says, "I see songwriting as having to do with experience, and the more you've experienced [in life], the better [your songwriting] is." He is still writing songs almost sixty years after his first hit.

The Rolling Stones had big hits even early on in the band's career.

Exciting Partnerships

Styles writes most of the songs he performs. He started writing when he was in One Direction. He wrote three songs for the band's debut album, *Up All Night*. For his solo albums, Styles has written or co-written almost every song. He often writes songs with different people. One of Styles's favorite collaborators is Kid Harpoon, who co-wrote and co-produced Styles's third album, *Harry's House*. The pair wrote some of the songs in a hotel room in Japan, using just a microphone, some guitars, and a laptop.

Styles's favorite instrument for writing songs is the guitar.

COOL CONNECTIONS

Both Jagger and Styles like to write their songs using an acoustic guitar. Strumming the guitar lets them experiment with different melodies to accompany their lyrics.

Being Honest

Styles has also written songs for other artists. He and his friend Johan Carlsson wrote "Just A Little Bit of Your Heart" for Ariana Grande. Styles thinks it is important that his songs tell the story of his life. When he left One Direction, he knew his solo songs had to be different. "I wanted to write my stories, things that happened to me. The number-one thing was I wanted to be honest," he said.

CHAPTER 3

On Stage!

Styles puts a lot of energy into his live shows. He follows the example set by his much older inspiration, Mick Jagger.

For more than six decades, the Rolling Stones have wowed their fans with their live shows. Much of the excitement is thanks to Jagger's amazing stage performances. He's famous for dancing in a way that is half-kicking and half-strutting.

Jagger has to be very fit to run across the stage and sing at the same time. He can run up to 12 miles (19.3 km) in a single concert. To keep in shape, he runs 8 miles (12.9 km) every morning. He also swims, cycles, and kickboxes.

Jagger's bold clothing choices make it easier for the audience to see him.

Styles's stage clothes make him instantly recognizable.

Jagger sometimes wears specially made clothes to stand out on stage.

Attention-Grabbing

Jagger is also famous for his stage clothes. He loves bright colors and has worn everything from jumpsuits to sequins. Men wearing makeup isn't always popular. But Jagger often appears on stage wearing eyeliner.

His appearance has changed over the years, but he still makes sure to grab people's attention. "Playing in a 15,000-seat arena, you have to cut more of a dash," Jagger says. He deliberately chooses a scarf or hat to make it easy for the audience to follow him.

Filling the Stage

Harry Styles performs on stage with a backing band and dancers. He often plays the acoustic guitar while he sings. Like Jagger, he is also known for his energy as a dancer.

Where Jagger runs around, however, Styles often takes part in elaborate routines with his dancers. The routines fill the stage, so fans have something exciting and dynamic to watch. To keep fit enough to perform, Styles runs and lifts weights. He is also a big fan of Pilates, a form of exercise done on a floor mat.

Styles plays a number of different acoustic guitars on stage.

For Love on Tour, Styles played 169 concerts around the world from 2021 to 2023.

Style Icon

Styles's stage clothes include skin-tight, brightly colored sequin jumpsuits. He often wears a feather boa around his neck. Styles surprises his audience every time. Sometimes, he will appear dressed up in a jacket and tie. Another time he might wear a dress, something that Jagger has also done on stage. Styles's bold clothing choices have helped him become a style icon.

COOL CONNECTIONS

Both Jagger and Styles embrace gender fluidity. Gender fluidity is when a person's gender identity is not fixed. A person can be male, female, or nonbinary, and switch between these.

CHAPTER 4

Enjoying Success

Mick Jagger has been performing for sixty years. Styles's career is a lot shorter. But both men have achieved great success and won many awards.

Jagger's long career is filled with many achievements. In 1989, he was inducted into the Rock and Roll Hall of Fame with the Rolling Stones. The band has also won two Grammy awards. In 2003, Jagger was knighted for his services to music. Queen Elizabeth II gave him an honorary title and named him Sir Mick Jagger.

From playing in small clubs to filling the world's largest stadiums, Jagger has seen it all. The Rolling Stones are still performing. They started their North American tour in 2024.

The Rolling Stones entered the Hall of Fame at the same time as performers Bruce Springsteen and Stevie Wonder.

Although Jagger turned eighty years old in 2023, he had no plans to quit performing. He said, "I enjoy going out there on stage and doing my stuff. That is what I do. I want everyone to enjoy themselves and forget the troubles in their lives for a couple of hours and just chill out."

Mick Jagger celebrated his eightieth birthday with a party attended by many celebrities.

COOL CONNECTIONS

In Great Britain, musicians vote for the winner of the Ivor Novello Award for best songwriting. Both Harry Styles and Mick Jagger have won the award.

Smashing Records

Harry Styles's career continues to smash records. With One Direction, Styles had four number one albums. Since going solo in 2017, he has released several albums. His third album, *Harry's House*, was released in 2022. It won three Grammys. His song "As it Was" was the most streamed song in twenty-four hours on Spotify.

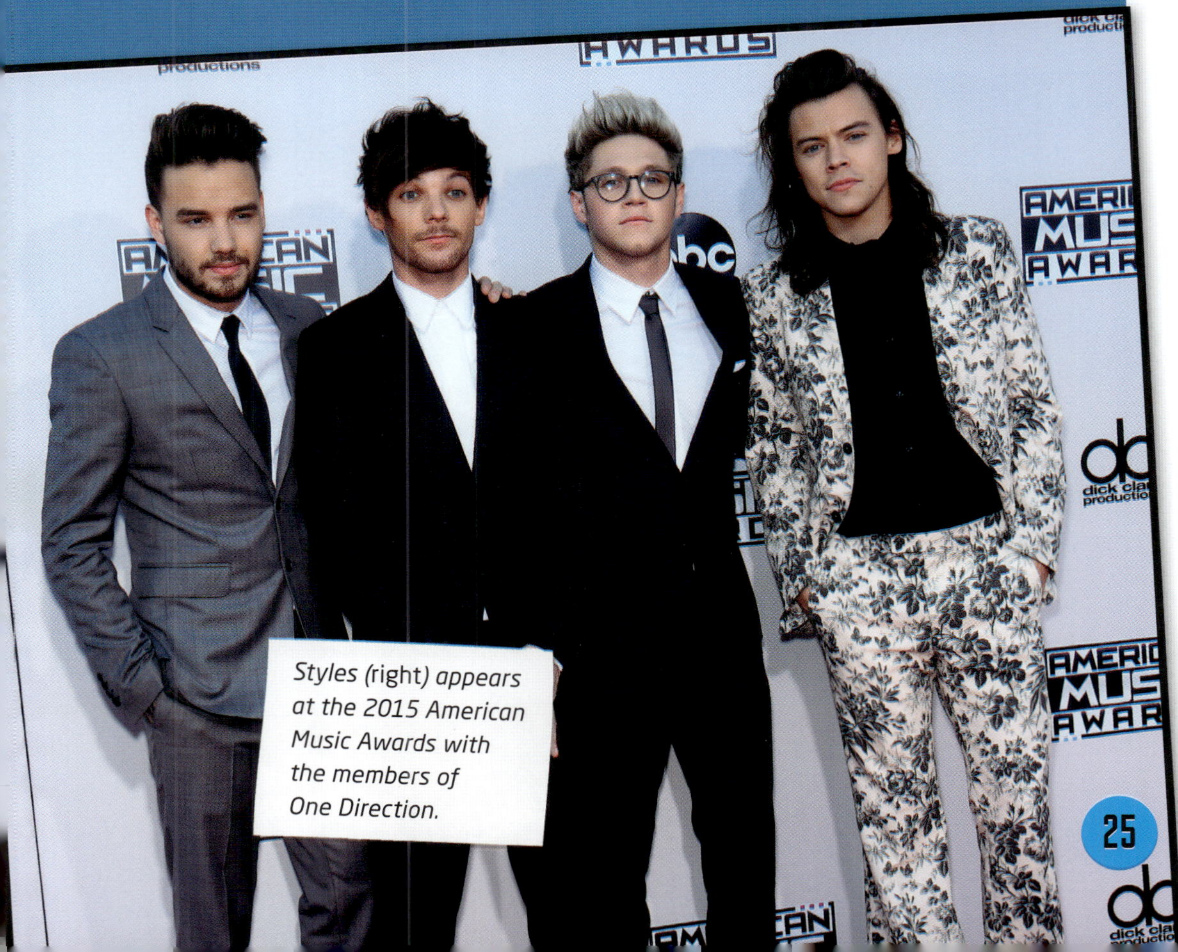

Styles (right) appears at the 2015 American Music Awards with the members of One Direction.

Setting an Example

Outside of music, Styles has broken down social barriers. He was the first man to appear on the cover of the women's fashion magazine *Vogue*, when he wore a gown. Being inclusive and allowing people to be themselves is at the heart of Styles's popularity. He often donates money from his concerts to charities.

On stage, he talks about equal rights and gender equality. In 2018, he launched a campaign called Treat People with Kindness. It encourages everyone to be accepting and inclusive of others.

Despite all his success, Harry Styles still looks up to his inspiration. He says that Mick Jagger is the "coolest man on the planet."

Styles regularly plays in exhibition soccer games to support charities.

Your Inspiration

When Jagger started out with the Rolling Stones in the 1960s, he just wanted to sing. Over the years, he has broken down social barriers. He is not afraid to dress differently, wear makeup, or be himself. He has inspired Styles to continually challenge set ideas of how people should look and act. Styles speaks out frequently about the importance of equal rights for everyone, no matter their color, race, or gender. He has shown us how important role models are in our daily lives.

Who inspires you? They don't have to be someone famous. It could be anyone: your best friend, your teacher, your aunt, or a person in your community. Why do they inspire you? What can you learn from them?

IMPORTANT DATES

1962 Mick Jagger reunites with his friend Keith Richards. They start the Rolling Stones.

1965 The Rolling Stones hit their first US number one on the charts with "(I Can't Get No) Satisfaction."

1989 Jagger and the Rolling Stones are inducted in the Rock and Roll Hall of Fame.

2003 Jagger is knighted for his services to music.

2010 Harry Styles auditions for *The X Factor*. He forms One Direction with four other members.

2011-15 One Direction becomes the biggest boy band in the world.

2017 Styles launches his solo career. He appears on *Saturday Night Live* as Mick Jagger.

2022 Styles releases his third album, *Harry's House*.

2023 Jagger turns eighty. Styles finishes his tour Love on Tour.

GLOSSARY

blues: a type of folk music created by African Americans in the early 20th century that began in the south
boa: a long, fluffy scarf
boy band: a pop group made up of young men who sing and dance, often appealing to a younger audience
collaborator: a person who works together on a task
debut: someone's first appearance in public in a particular role
elaborate: having many complicated parts
inclusive: including everyone
lyric: the words of a song
opening act: a performer who appears in a concert before the main act
sequin: a small, shiny disk sewn onto clothes for decoration
solo: performing on their own

SOURCE NOTES

5 Daniel Kreps, "Mick Jagger on Harry Styles: 'Superficial Resemblance to My Younger Self,'" *Rolling Stone*, May 22, 2022, https://www.rollingstone.com/music/music-news/mick-jagger-harry-styles-superficial-resemblance-1356889/.

12 "Mick Jagger and Keith Richards," ABKCO Music and Records, https://www.abkco.com/songwriter/mick-jagger-keith-richards songwriter-info-credits-bio/.

15 Cameron Crowe, "Harry Styles' New Direction," *Rolling Stone*, April 18, 2017, https://www.rollingstone.com/feature/harry-styles-new-direction-119432/.

18 Tim Blanks, "Mick Jagger on the Outfits that Have Helped Him Shapeshift Through the Ages," *Another Man*, July 26, 2018, https://www.anothermanmag.com/life-culture/10432/mick-jagger-on-the-outfits-that-have-helped-him-shapeshift-through-the-ages.

24 "Mick Jagger Opens Up About Retiring and the Artists Who Bring 'a Bit of Life to Rock and Roll,'" *Virgin Radio UK*, April 25, 2022, https://virginradio.co.uk/music/58677/mick-jagger-opens-up-about-retiring-and-the-artists-who-bring-a-bit-of-life-to-rock-and-roll.

26 Stephen Doig, "Move Over Harry Styles—Old Rockers Do Fashion Best," *The Telegraph*, September 18, 2022, https://www.telegraph.co.uk/fashion/style/move-harry-styles-old rockers-do-fashion-best/.

LEARN MORE

Anderson, Kirsten. *Who Is Harry Styles?* New York: Penguin Workshop, 2023.

Andrews, Elizabeth. *Harry Styles: Everyone's Favorite Performer*. Minneapolis: ABDO, 2023.

Britannica Kids: Harry Styles
https://kids.britannica.com/students/article/Harry-Styles/635493

Britannica Kids: the Rolling Stones
https://kids.britannica.com/students/article/the-Rolling-Stones/276771

Huddleston, Emma. *Harry Styles*. Lake Elmo, MN: Focus Readers, 2021.

Kiddle: Harry Styles Facts for Kids
https://kids.kiddle.co/Harry_Styles

Kiddle: Mick Jagger Facts for Kids
https://kids.kiddle.co/Mick_Jagger

Schwartz, Heather E. *Harry Styles: Chart-Topping Musician and Style Icon*. Minneapolis: Lerner Publications, 2024.

INDEX

PHOTO ACKNOWLEDGMENTS

Image credits: @foto.grafinhas/Instagram, p. 4; Jerry Coli/Dreamstime.com, p. 5; Stefano Chiacchiarini '74/Shutterstock.com, pp. 7a, 13a; Featureflash Photo Agency/Shutterstock.com, p. 7b; Fabio Diena/Dreamstime.com, p. 8; Andrea Raffin/Shutterstock.com, p. 9; fokke baarssen/Shutterstock.com, p. 10a; Fred Duval/Shutterstock.com, p. 10b; Skyhawk/Shutterstock.com, p. 11a Gyvafoto/Shutterstock.com, p. 11b; Boggy/Dreamstime.com, p. 11c; sorayut/Shutterstock.com, p. 13b; Vladvm/Shutterstock.com, p. 13c; PV Productions/Shutterstock.com, p. 13d; sunny feet/Dreamstime.com, p. 14; robert_s/Shutterstock.com, p. 15; Nationaal Archief/Wikimedia Commons, p. 17a; Lovclyhes/Wikimedia Commons, p. 17b; Ben Houdijk/Shutterstock.com, p. 18; lev radin/Shutterstock.com, p. 19; Lily Redman/Flickr.com, p. 20a; lev radin/Shutterstock.com, p. 20b; Michael715/Shutterstock.com, p. 20c; f11 photo/Shutterstock.com, p. 23a; Bruce Alan Bennett/Shutterstock.com, p. 23b; Raph_PH/Wikimedia Commons, p. 24; DFree/Shutterstock.com, p. 25; vagueonthehow/Wikimedia Commons, p. 26. Cover: Ben Houdijk/Shutterstock.com; D Wong/Dreamstime.com.